WALT WHITMAN
I HEAR AMERICA SINGING

Walt Whitman

I Hear America Singing

Poems of Democracy, Manhattan,
and the Future

ANVIL PRESS POETRY

Published in 2001
by Anvil Press Poetry Ltd
Neptune House 70 Royal Hill London SE10 8RF
www.anvilpresspoetry.com

This book is published with financial assistance
from The Arts Council of England

ISBN 0 85646 340 X

Designed and set in Monotype Ehrhardt by Anvil
Printed in the United States of America
by Boyd Printing Company, Albany, NY

PREFACE

THIS BRIEF SELECTION of courageous and consoling poems, spanning the whole of Whitman's writing career, focuses on his vision of democracy, his love of cities (especially Manhattan), his sense of the future – and of the community of peoples of this earth. His unwavering belief in the democratic values around which the States united in his time is salutary – and heartening.

Whitman's writing, with its openness, expansiveness, delight in humanity at large ('en-masse') and its passionate moral courage, is profoundly reassuring. His empathy with all conditions of people, and his visionary – even prophetic – sense of the reality of the American dream make him as much a poet for our time as he was for the time of the American Civil War and its aftermath.

With the exception of the final three poems which were collected in the 1897 edition, the poems are chosen from the final edition of *Leaves of Grass* (1891-2) authorized by the poet at the end of his life, and are printed in the same order.

THE PUBLISHER

I am the man, I suffer'd, I was there . . .

* * *

I am the mash'd fireman with breast-bone broken,
Tumbling walls buried me in their debris,
Heat and smoke I inspired, I heard the yelling shouts of
*   my comrades,*
I heard the distant click of their picks and shovels,
They have clear'd the beams away, they tenderly lift
*   me forth.*

SONG OF MYSELF, 33

CONTENTS

ONE'S-SELF I SING

One's-Self I sing, a simple separate person,
Yet utter the word Democratic, the word En-Masse.

Of physiology from top to toe I sing,
Not physiognomy alone nor brain alone is worthy for the
    Muse, I say the Form complete is worthier far,
The Female equally with the Male I sing.

Of Life immense in passion, pulse, and power,
Cheerful, for freest action form'd under the laws divine,
The Modern Man I sing.

TO FOREIGN LANDS

I heard that you ask'd for something to prove this puzzle the
    New World,
And to define America, her athletic Democracy,
Therefore I send you my poems that you behold in them
    what you wanted.

TO A HISTORIAN

You who celebrate bygones,
Who have explored the outward, the surfaces of the races,
    the life that has exhibited itself,
Who have treated of man as the creature of politics, aggre-
    gates, rulers and priests,
I, habitan of the Alleghanies, treating of him as he is in
    himself in his own rights,
Pressing the pulse of the life that has seldom exhibited itself,
    (the great pride of man in himself,)
Chanter of Personality, outlining what is yet to be,
I project the history of the future.

How they are provided for upon the earth, (appearing at
    intervals,)
How dear and dreadful they are to the earth,
How they inure to themselves as much as to any – what a
    paradox appears their age,
How people respond to them, yet know them not,
How there is something relentless in their fate all times,
How all times mischoose the objects of their adulation and
    reward,
And how the same inexorable price must still be paid for the
    same great purchase.

TO THE STATES

To the States or any one of them, or any city of the States,
    Resist much, obey little,
Once unquestioning obedience, once fully enslaved,
Once fully enslaved, no nation, state, city of this earth, ever
    afterward resumes its liberty.

I HEAR AMERICA SINGING

I hear America singing, the varied carols I hear,
Those of mechanics, each one singing his as it should be
    blithe and strong,
The carpenter singing his as he measures his plank or beam,
The mason singing his as he makes ready for work, or leaves
    off work,
The boatman singing what belongs to him in his boat, the
    deckhand singing on the steamboat deck,
The shoemaker singing as he sits on his bench, the hatter
    singing as he stands,
The wood-cutter's song, the ploughboy's on his way in the
    morning, or at noon intermission or at sundown,
The delicious singing of the mother, or of the young wife
    at work, or of the girl sewing or washing,
Each singing what belongs to him or her and to none else,
The day what belongs to the day – at night the party of
    young fellows, robust, friendly,
Singing with open mouths their strong melodious songs.

WHAT PLACE IS BESIEGED?

What place is besieged, and vainly tries to raise the siege?
Lo, I send to that place a commander, swift, brave, immortal,
And with him horse and foot, and parks of artillery,
And artillery-men, the deadliest that ever fired gun.

POETS TO COME

Poets to come! orators, singers, musicians to come!
Not to-day is to justify me and answer what I am for,
But you, a new brood, native, athletic, continental, greater
    than before known,
Arouse! for you must justify me.

I myself but write one or two indicative words for the
    future,
I but advance a moment only to wheel and hurry back in
    the darkness.

I am a man who, sauntering along without fully stopping,
    turns a casual look upon you and then averts his face,
Leaving it to you to prove and define it,
Expecting the main things from you.

12

Democracy! near at hand to you a throat is now inflating
    itself and joyfully singing.

Ma femme! for the brood beyond us and of us,
For those who belong here and those to come,
I exultant to be ready for them will now shake out carols
    stronger and haughtier than have ever yet been heard
    upon earth.

I will make the songs of passion to give them their way,
And your songs outlaw'd offenders, for I scan you with
    kindred eyes, and carry you with me the same as any.

I will make the true poem of riches,
To earn for the body and the mind whatever adheres and
    goes forward and is not dropt by death;
I will effuse egotism and show it underlying all, and I will be
    the bard of personality,
And I will show of male and female that either is but the
    equal of the other,
And sexual organs and acts! do you concentrate in me, for I
    am determin'd to tell you with courageous clear voice
    to prove you illustrious,
And I will show that there is no imperfection in the present,
    and can be none in the future,
And I will show that whatever happens to anybody it may be
    turn'd to beautiful results,
And I will show that nothing can happen more beautiful
    than death,

And I will thread a thread through my poems that time and
     events are compact,
And that all the things of the universe are perfect miracles,
     each as profound as any.

I will not make poems with reference to parts,
But I will make poems, songs, thoughts, with reference to
     ensemble,
And I will not sing with reference to a day, but with reference
     to all days,
And I will not make a poem nor the least part of a poem but
     has reference to the soul,
Because having look'd at the objects of the universe, I find
     there is no one nor any particle of one but has reference
     to the soul.

FOR YOU O DEMOCRACY

Come, I will make the continent indissoluble,
I will make the most splendid race the sun ever shone upon,
I will make divine magnetic lands,
   With the love of comrades,
    With the life-long love of comrades.

I will plant companionship thick as trees along all the rivers
  of America, and along the shores of the great lakes, and
  all over the prairies,
I will make inseparable cities with their arms about each
  other's necks,
   By the love of comrades,
    By the manly love of comrades.

For you these from me, O Democracy, to serve you ma femme!
For you, for you I am trilling these songs.

City of orgies, walks and joys,
City whom that I have lived and sung in your midst will one
    day make you illustrious,
Not the pageants of you, not your shifting tableaus, your
    spectacles, repay me,
Not the interminable rows of your houses, nor the ships at
    the wharves,
Nor the processions in the streets, nor the bright windows
    with goods in them,
Nor to converse with learn'd persons, or bear my share in
    the soiree or feast;
Not those, but as I pass O Manhattan, your frequent and
    swift flash of eyes offering me love,
Offering response to my own – these repay me,
Lovers, continual lovers, only repay me.

I DREAM'D IN A DREAM

I dream'd in a dream I saw a city invincible to the attacks
    of the whole of the rest of the earth,
I dream'd that was the new city of Friends,
Nothing was greater there than the quality of robust love,
    it led the rest,
It was seen every hour in the actions of the men of that city,
And in all their looks and words.

SALUT AU MONDE!

1

O take my hand Walt Whitman!
Such gliding wonders! such sights and sounds!
Such join'd unended links, each hook'd to the next,
Each answering all, each sharing the earth with all.

What widens within you Walt Whitman?
What waves and soils exuding?
What climes? what persons and cities are here?
Who are the infants, some playing, some slumbering?
Who are the girls? who are the married women?
Who are the groups of old men going slowly with their arms
      about each other's necks?
What rivers are these? what forests and fruits are these?
What are the mountains call'd that rise so high in the mists?
What myriads of dwellings are they fill'd with dwellers?

2

Within me latitude widens, longitude lengthens,
Asia, Africa, Europe, are to the east – America is provided
      for in the west,
Banding the bulge of the earth winds the hot equator,
Curiously north and south turn the axis-ends,
Within me is the longest day, the sun wheels in slanting
      rings, it does not set for months,
Stretch'd in due time within me the midnight sun just rises
      above the horizon and sinks again,
Within me zones, seas, cataracts, forests, volcanoes, groups,
Malaysia, Polynesia, and the great West Indian islands.

3

What do you hear Walt Whitman?

I hear the workman singing and the farmer's wife singing,
I hear in the distance the sounds of children and of animals
   early in the day,
I hear emulous shouts of Australians pursuing the wild
   horse,
I hear the Spanish dance with castanets in the chestnut
   shade, to the rebeck and guitar,
I hear continual echoes from the Thames,
I hear fierce French liberty songs,
I hear of the Italian boat-sculler the musical recitative of old
   poems,
I hear the locusts in Syria as they strike the grain and grass
   with the showers of their terrible clouds,
I hear the Coptic refrain toward sundown, pensively falling
   on the breast of the black venerable vast mother the Nile,
I hear the chirp of the Mexican muleteer, and the bells of
   the mule,
I hear the Arab muezzin calling from the top of the mosque,
I hear the Christian priests at the altars of their churches,
   I hear the responsive base and soprano,
I hear the cry of the Cossack, and the sailor's voice putting
   to sea at Okotsk,
I hear the wheeze of the slave-coffle as the slaves march on,
   as the husky gangs pass on by twos and threes, fasten'd
   together with wrist-chains and ankle-chains,
I hear the Hebrew reading his records and psalms,
I hear the rhythmic myths of the Greeks, and the strong
   legends of the Romans,

I hear the tale of the divine life and bloody death of the beautiful God the Christ,

I hear the Hindoo teaching his favorite pupil the loves, wars, adages, transmitted safely to this day from poets who wrote three thousand years ago.

4

What do you see Walt Whitman?

Who are they you salute, and that one after another salute you?

I see a great round wonder rolling through space,

I see diminute farms, hamlets, ruins, graveyards, jails, factories, palaces, hovels, huts of barbarians, tents of nomads upon the surface,

I see the shaded part on one side where the sleepers are sleeping, and the sunlit part on the other side,

I see the curious rapid change of the light and shade,

I see distant lands, as real and near to the inhabitants of them as my land is to me.

I see plenteous waters,

I see mountain peaks, I see the sierras of Andes where they range,

I see plainly the Himalayas, Chian Shahs, Altays, Ghauts,

I see the giant pinnacles of Elbruz, Kazbek, Bazardjusi,

I see the Styrian Alps, and the Karnac Alps,

I see the Pyrenees, Balks, Carpathians, and to the north the Dofrafields, and off at sea mount Hecla,

I see Vesuvius and Etna, the mountains of the Moon, and the Red mountains of Madagascar,

I see the Lybian, Arabian, and Asiatic deserts,

I see huge dreadful Arctic and Antarctic icebergs,
I see the superior oceans and the inferior ones, the Atlantic
and Pacific, the sea of Mexico, the Brazilian sea, and
the sea of Peru,
The waters of Hindustan, the China sea, and the gulf of
Guinea,
The Japan waters, the beautiful bay of Nagasaki land-lock'd
in its mountains,
The spread of the Baltic, Caspian, Bothnia, the British
shores, and the bay of Biscay,
The clear-sunn'd Mediterranean, and from one to another
of its islands,
The White sea, and the sea around Greenland.

I behold the mariners of the world,
Some are in storms, some in the night with the watch on the
look-out,
Some drifting helplessly, some with contagious diseases.

I behold the sail and steamships of the world, some in clusters
in port, some on their voyages,
Some double the cape of Storms, some cape Verde, others
capes Guardafui, Bon, or Bajadore,
Others Dondra head, others pass the straits of Sunda,
others cape Lopatka, others Behring's straits,
Others cape Horn, others sail the gulf of Mexico or along
Cuba or Hayti, others Hudson's bay or Baffin's bay,
Others pass the straits of Dover, others enter the Wash,
others the firth of Solway, others round cape Clear,
others the Land's End,
Others traverse the Zuyder Zee or the Scheld,
Others as comers and goers at Gibraltar or the Dardanelles,

Others sternly push their way through the northern winter-
packs,
Others descend or ascend the Obi or the Lena,
Others the Niger or the Congo, others the Indus, the
Burampooter and Cambodia,
Others wait steam'd up ready to start in the ports of
Australia,
Wait at Liverpool, Glasgow, Dublin, Marseilles, Lisbon,
Naples, Hamburg, Bremen, Bordeaux, the Hague,
Copenhagen,
Wait at Valparaiso, Rio Janeiro, Panama.

5

I see the tracks of the railroads of the earth,
I see them in Great Britain, I see them in Europe,
I see them in Asia and in Africa.

I see the electric telegraphs of the earth,
I see the filaments of the news of the wars, deaths, losses,
gains, passions, of my race.

I see the long river-stripes of the earth,
I see the Amazon and the Paraguay,
I see the four great rivers of China, the Amour, the Yellow
River, the Yiang-tse, and the Pearl,
I see where the Seine flows, and where the Danube, the
Loire, the Rhone, and the Guadalquiver flow,
I see the windings of the Volga, the Dnieper, the Oder,
I see the Tuscan going down the Arno, and the Venetian
along the Po,
I see the Greek seaman sailing out of Egina bay.

6

I see the site of the old empire of Assyria, and that of Persia,
    and that of India,
I see the falling of the Ganges over the high rim of Saukara.

I see the place of the idea of the Deity incarnated by avatars
    in human forms,
I see the spots of the successions of priests on the earth,
    oracles, sacrificers, brahmins, sabians, llamas, monks,
    muftis, exhorters,
I see where druids walk'd the groves of Mona, I see the
    mistletoe and vervain,
I see the temples of the deaths of the bodies of Gods, I see
    the old signifiers.

I see Christ eating the bread of his last supper in the midst
    of youths and old persons,
I see where the strong divine young man the Hercules toil'd
    faithfully and long and then died,
I see the place of the innocent rich life and hapless fate of
    the beautiful nocturnal son, the full-limb'd Bacchus,
I see Kneph, blooming, drest in blue, with the crown of
    feathers on his head,
I see Hermes, unsuspected, dying, well-belov'd, saying to
    the people *Do not weep for me,*
This is not my true country, I have lived banish'd from my true
    country, I now go back there,
I return to the celestial sphere where every one goes in his turn.

7

I see the battle-fields of the earth, grass grows upon them
    and blossoms and corn,
I see the tracks of ancient and modern expeditions.

I see the nameless masonries, venerable messages of the
    unknown events, heroes, records of the earth.

I see the places of the sagas,
I see pine-trees and fir-trees torn by northern blasts,
I see granite bowlders and cliffs, I see green meadows and
    lakes,
I see the burial-cairns of Scandinavian warriors,
I see them raised high with stones by the marge of restless
    oceans, that the dead men's spirits when they wearied of
    their quiet graves might rise up through the mounds
    and gaze on the tossing billows, and be refresh'd by
    storms, immensity, liberty, action.

I see the steppes of Asia,
I see the tumuli of Mongolia, I see the tents of Kalmucks
    and Baskirs,
I see the nomadic tribes with herds of oxen and cows,
I see the table-lands notch'd with ravines, I see the jungles
    and deserts,
I see the camel, the wild steed, the bustard, the fat-tail'd
    sheep, the antelope, and the burrowing wolf.

I see the highlands of Abyssinia,
I see flocks of goats feeding, and see the fig-tree, tamarind,
    date,
And see fields of teff-wheat and places of verdure and gold.

I see the Brazilian vaquero,
I see the Bolivian ascending mount Sorata,
I see the Wacho crossing the plains, I see the incomparable
rider of horses with his lasso on his arm,
I see over the pampas the pursuit of wild cattle for their
hides.

8

I see the regions of snow and ice,
I see the sharp-eyed Samoiede and the Finn,
I see the seal-seeker in his boat poising his lance,
I see the Siberian on his slight-built sledge drawn by dogs,
I see the porpoise-hunters, I see the whale-crews of the
south Pacific and the north Atlantic,
I see the cliffs, glaciers, torrents, valleys, of Switzerland – I
mark the long winters and the isolation.

9

I see the cities of the earth and make myself at random
a part of them,
I am a real Parisian,
I am a habitan of Vienna, St. Petersburg, Berlin, Constan-
tinople,
I am of Adelaide, Sidney, Melbourne,
I am of London, Manchester, Bristol, Edinburgh, Limerick,
I am of Madrid, Cadiz, Barcelona, Oporto, Lyons, Brussels,
Berne, Frankfort, Stuttgart, Turin, Florence,
I belong in Moscow, Cracow, Warsaw, or northward in
Christiania or Stockholm, or in Siberian Irkutsk, or in
some street in Iceland,
I descend upon all those cities, and rise from them again.

I see vapors exhaling from unexplored countries,
I see the savage types, the bow and arrow, the poison'd
    splint, the fetich, and the obi.

I see African and Asiatic towns,
I see Algiers, Tripoli, Derne, Mogadore, Timbuctoo,
    Monrovia,
I see the swarms of Pekin, Canton, Benares, Delhi,
    Calcutta, Tokio,
I see the Kruman in his hut, and the Dahoman and
    Ashantee-man in their huts,
I see the Turk smoking opium in Aleppo,
I see the picturesque crowds at the fairs of Khiva and those
    of Herat,
I see Teheran, I see Muscat and Medina and the intervening
    sands, I see the caravans toiling onward,
I see Egypt and the Egyptians, I see the pyramids and
    obelisks,
I look on chisell'd histories, records of conquering kings,
    dynasties, cut in slabs of sand-stone, or on granite-
    blocks,
I see at Memphis mummy-pits containing mummies
    embalm'd, swathed in linen cloth, lying there many
    centuries,
I look on the fall'n Theban, the large-ball'd eyes, the side-
    drooping neck, the hands folded across the breast.

I see all the menials of the earth, laboring,
I see all the prisoners in the prisons,
I see the defective human bodies of the earth,
The blind, the deaf and dumb, idiots, hunchbacks, lunatics,

The pirates, thieves, betrayers, murderers, slave-makers of
　　the earth,
The helpless infants, and the helpless old men and women.

I see male and female everywhere,
I see the serene brotherhood of philosophs,
I see the constructiveness of my race,
I see the results of the perseverance and industry of my
　　race,
I see ranks, colors, barbarisms, civilizations, I go among
　　them, I mix indiscriminately,
And I salute all the inhabitants of the earth.

11

You whoever you are!
You daughter or son of England!
You of the mighty Slavic tribes and empires! you Russ in
　　Russia!
You dim-descended, black, divine-soul'd African, large,
　　fine-headed, nobly-form'd, superbly destin'd, on equal
　　terms with me!
You Norwegian! Swede! Dane! Icelander! you Prussian!
You Spaniard of Spain! you Portuguese!
You Frenchwoman and Frenchman of France!
You Belge! you liberty-lover of the Netherlands! (you stock
　　whence I myself have descended;)
You sturdy Austrian! you Lombard! Hun! Bohemian!
　　farmer of Styria!
Yon neighbor of the Danube!
You working-man of the Rhine, the Elbe, or the Weser! you
　　working-woman too!
You Sardinian! you Bavarian! Swabian! Saxon! Wallachian!
　　Bulgarian!

You Roman! Neapolitan! you Greek!

You lithe matador in the arena at Seville!

You mountaineer living lawlessly on the Taurus or Caucasus!

You Bokh horse-herd watching your mares and stallions feeding!

You beautiful-bodied Persian at full speed in the saddle shooting arrows to the mark!

You Chinaman and Chinawoman of China! you Tartar of Tartary!

You women of the earth subordinated at your tasks!

You Jew journeying in your old age through every risk to stand once on Syrian ground!

You other Jews waiting in all lands for your Messiah!

You thoughtful Armenian pondering by some stream of the Euphrates! you peering amid the ruins of Nineveh! you ascending mount Ararat!

You foot-worn pilgrim welcoming the far-away sparkle of the minarets of Mecca!

You sheiks along the stretch from Suez to Bab-el-mandeb ruling your families and tribes!

You olive-grower tending your fruit on fields of Nazareth, Damascus, or lake Tiberias!

You Thibet trader on the wide inland or bargaining in the shops of Lassa!

You Japanese man or woman! you liver in Madagascar, Ceylon, Sumatra, Borneo!

All you continentals of Asia, Africa, Europe, Australia, indifferent of place!

All you on the numberless islands of the archipelagoes of the sea!

And you of centuries hence when you listen to me!

And you each and everywhere whom I specify not, but
   include just the same!
Health to you! good will to you all, from me and America
   sent!

Each of us inevitable,
Each of us limitless – each of us with his or her right upon
   the earth,
Each of us allow'd the eternal purports of the earth,
Each of us here as divinely as any is here.

12

You Hottentot with clicking palate! you woolly-hair'd
   hordes!
You own'd persons dropping sweat-drops or blood-drops!
You human forms with the fathomless ever-impressive
   countenances of brutes!
You poor koboo whom the meanest of the rest look down
   upon for all your glimmering language and spirituality!
You dwarf'd Kamtschatkan, Greenlander, Lapp!
You Austral negro, naked, red, sooty, with protrusive lip,
   groveling, seeking your food!
You Caffre, Berber, Soudanese!
You haggard, uncouth, untutor'd Bedowee!
You plague-swarms in Madras, Nankin, Kaubul, Cairo!
You benighted roamer of Amazonia! you Patagonian! you
   Feejeeman!
I do not prefer others so very much before you either,
I do not say one word against you, away back there where
   you stand,
(You will come forward in due time to my side.)

13

My spirit has pass'd in compassion and determination
    around the whole earth,
I have look'd for equals and lovers and found them ready
    for me in all lands,
I think some divine rapport has equalized me with them.

You vapors, I think I have risen with you, moved away to
    distant continents, and fallen down there, for reasons,
I think I have blown with you you winds;
You waters I have finger'd every shore with you,
I have run through what any river or strait of the globe has
    run through,
I have taken my stand on the bases of peninsulas and on the
    high embedded rocks, to cry thence:

Salut au monde!
What cities the light or warmth penetrates I penetrate those
    cities myself,
All islands to which birds wing their way I wing my way
    myself.

Toward you all, in America's name,
I raise high the perpendicular hand, I make the signal,
To remain after me in sight forever,
For all the haunts and homes of men.

CROSSING BROOKLYN FERRY

1

Flood-tide below me! I see you face to face!
Clouds of the west – sun there half an hour high – I see you
  also face to face.

Crowds of men and women attired in the usual costumes,
  how curious you are to me!
On the ferry-boats the hundreds and hundreds that cross,
  returning home, are more curious to me than you
  suppose,
And you that shall cross from shore to shore years hence are
  more to me, and more in my meditations, than you
  might suppose.

2

The impalpable sustenance of me from all things at all
  hours of the day,
The simple, compact, well-join'd scheme, myself disinte-
  grated, every one disintegrated yet part of the scheme,
The similitudes of the past and those of the future,
The glories strung like beads on my smallest sights and
  hearings, on the walk in the street and the passage over
  the river,
The current rushing so swiftly and swimming with me far
  away,
The others that are to follow me, the ties between me and
  them,
The certainty of others, the life, love, sight, hearing of
  others.

Others will enter the gates of the ferry and cross from shore
    to shore,
Others will watch the run of the flood-tide,
Others will see the shipping of Manhattan north and west,
    and the heights of Brooklyn to the south and east,
Others will see the islands large and small;
Fifty years hence, others will see them as they cross, the sun
    half an hour high,
A hundred years hence, or ever so many hundred years
    hence, others will see them,
Will enjoy the sunset, the pouring-in of the flood-tide, the
    falling-back to the sea of the ebb-tide.

3

It avails not, time nor place – distance avails not,
I am with you, you men and women of a generation, or ever
    so many generations hence,
Just as you feel when you look on the river and sky, so I felt,
Just as any of you is one of a living crowd, I was one of a
    crowd,
Just as you are refresh'd by the gladness of the river and the
    bright flow, I was refresh'd,
Just as you stand and lean on the rail, yet hurry with the
    swift current, I stood yet was hurried,
Just as you look on the numberless masts of ships and the
    thick-stemm'd pipes of steamboats, I look'd.

I too many and many a time cross'd the river of old,
Watched the Twelfth-month sea-gulls, saw them high in
    the air floating with motionless wings, oscillating their
    bodies,
Saw how the glistening yellow lit up parts of their bodies
    and left the rest in strong shadow,

Saw the slow-wheeling circles and the gradual edging
    toward the south,
Saw the reflection of the summer sky in the water,
Had my eyes dazzled by the shimmering track of beams,
Look'd at the fine centrifugal spokes of light round the
    shape of my head in the sunlit water,
Look'd on the haze on the hills southward and south-west-
    ward,
Look'd on the vapor as it flew in fleeces tinged with violet,
Look'd toward the lower bay to notice the vessels arriving,
Saw their approach, saw aboard those that were near me,
Saw the white sails of schooners and sloops, saw the ships
    at anchor,
The sailors at work in the rigging or out astride the spars,
The round masts, the swinging motion of the hulls, the
    slender serpentine pennants,
The large and small steamers in motion, the pilots in their
    pilot-houses,
The white wake left by the passage, the quick tremulous
    whirl of the wheels,
The flags of all nations, the falling of them at sunset,
The scallop-edged waves in the twilight, the ladled cups,
    the frolicsome crests and glistening,
The stretch afar growing dimmer and dimmer, the gray
    walls of the granite storehouses by the docks,
On the river the shadowy group, the big steam-tug closely
    flank'd on each side by the barges, the hay-boat, the
    belated lighter,
On the neighboring shore the fires from the foundry chimneys
    burning high and glaringly into the night,
Casting their flicker of black contrasted with wild red and
    yellow light over the tops of houses, and down into the
    clefts of streets.

4

These and all else were to me the same as they are to you,
I loved well those cities, loved well the stately and rapid
    river,
The men and women I saw were all near to me,
Others the same – others who look back on me because I
    look'd forward to them,
(The time will come, though I stop here to-day and to-
    night.)

5

What is it then between us?
What is the count of the scores or hundreds of years
    between us?

Whatever it is, it avails not – distance avails not, and place
    avails not,
I too lived, Brooklyn of ample hills was mine,
I too walk'd the streets of Manhattan island, and bathed in
    the waters around it,
I too felt the curious abrupt questionings stir within me,
In the day among crowds of people sometimes they came
    upon me,
In my walks home late at night or as I lay in my bed they
    came upon me,
I too had been struck from the float forever held in solution,
I too had receiv'd identity by my body,
That I was I knew was of my body, and what I should be
    I knew I should be of my body.

6

It is not upon you alone the dark patches fall,
The dark threw its patches down upon me also,
The best I had done seem'd to me blank and suspicious,
My great thoughts as I supposed them, were they not in
    reality meagre?
Nor is it you alone who know what it is to be evil,
I am he who knew what it was to be evil,
I too knitted the old knot of contrariety,
Blabb'd, blush'd, resented, lied, stole, grudg'd,
Had guile, anger, lust, hot wishes I dared not speak,
Was wayward, vain, greedy, shallow, sly, cowardly, malignant,
The wolf, the snake, the hog, not wanting in me,
The cheating look, the frivolous word, the adulterous wish,
    not wanting,
Refusals, hates, postponements, meanness, laziness, none of
    these wanting,
Was one with the rest, the days and haps of the rest,
Was call'd by my nighest name by clear loud voices of young
    men as they saw me approaching or passing,
Felt their arms on my neck as I stood, or the negligent
    leaning of their flesh against me as I sat,
Saw many I loved in the street or ferry-boat or public
    assembly, yet never told them a word,
Lived the same life with the rest, the same old laughing,
    gnawing, sleeping,
Play'd the part that still looks back on the actor or actress,
The same old role, the role that is what we make it, as great
    as we like,
Or as small as we like, or both great and small.

7

Closer yet I approach you,
What thought you have of me now, I had as much of you –
    I laid in my stores in advance,
I consider'd long and seriously of you before you were born.

Who was to know what should come home to me?
Who knows but I am enjoying this?
Who knows, for all the distance, but I am as good as looking
    at you now, for all you cannot see me?

8

Ah, what can ever be more stately and admirable to me than
    mast-hemm'd Manhattan?
River and sunset and scallop-edg'd waves of flood-tide?
The sea-gulls oscillating their bodies, the hay-boat in the
    twilight, and the belated lighter?
What gods can exceed these that clasp me by the hand, and
    with voices I love call me promptly and loudly by my
    nighest name as I approach?
What is more subtle than this which ties me to the woman
    or man that looks in my face?
Which fuses me into you now, and pours my meaning into
    you?

We understand then do we not?
What I promis'd without mentioning it, have you not
    accepted?
What the study could not teach – what the preaching could
    not accomplish is accomplish'd, is it not?

9

Flow on, river! flow with the flood-tide, and ebb with the
    ebb-tide!

Frolic on, crested and scallop-edg'd waves!

Gorgeous clouds of the sunset! drench with your splendor
    me, or the men and women generations after me!

Cross from shore to shore, countless crowds of passengers!

Stand up, tall masts of Mannahatta! stand up, beautiful
    hills of Brooklyn!

Throb, baffled and curious brain! throw out questions and
    answers!

Suspend here and everywhere, eternal float of solution!

Gaze, loving and thirsting eyes, in the house or street or
    public assembly!

Sound out, voices of young men! loudly and musically call
    me by my nighest name!

Live, old life! play the part that looks back on the actor or
    actress!

Play the old role, the role that is great or small according as
    one makes it!

Consider, you who peruse me, whether I may not in
    unknown ways be looking upon you;

Be firm, rail over the river, to support those who lean idly,
    yet haste with the hasting current;

Fly on, sea-birds! fly sideways, or wheel in large circles high
    in the air;

Receive the summer sky, you water, and faithfully hold it
    till all downcast eyes have time to take it from you!

Diverge, fine spokes of light, from the shape of my head, or
    any one's head, in the sunlit water!

Come on, ships from the lower bay! pass up or down, white-
    sail'd schooners, sloops, lighters!

Flaunt away, flags of all nations! be duly lower'd at sunset!

Burn high your fires, foundry chimneys! cast black shadows at nightfall! cast red and yellow light over the tops of the houses!

Appearances, now or henceforth, indicate what you are,

You necessary film, continue to envelop the soul,

About my body for me, and your body for you, be hung our divinest aromas,

Thrive, cities – bring your freight, bring your shows, ample and sufficient rivers,

Expand, being than which none else is perhaps more spiritual,

Keep your places, objects than which none else is more lasting.

You have waited, you always wait, you dumb, beautiful ministers,

We receive you with free sense at last, and are insatiate henceforward,

Not you any more shall be able to foil us, or withhold yourselves from us,

We use you, and do not cast you aside – we plant you permanently within us,

We fathom you not – we love you – there is perfection in you also,

You furnish your parts toward eternity,

Great or small, you furnish your parts toward the soul.

5

The place where a great city stands is not the place of
    stretch'd wharves, docks, manufactures, deposits of
    produce merely,
Nor the place of ceaseless salutes of new-comers or the
    anchor-lifters of the departing,
Nor the place of the tallest and costliest buildings or shops
    selling goods from the rest of the earth,
Nor the place of the best libraries and schools, nor the place
    where money is plentiest,
Nor the place of the most numerous population.

Where the city stands with the brawniest breed of orators
    and bards,
Where the city stands that is belov'd by these, and loves them
    in return and understands them,
Where no monuments exist to heroes but in the common
    words and deeds,
Where thrift is in its place, and prudence is in its place,
Where the men and women think lightly of the laws,
Where the slave ceases, and the master of slaves ceases,
Where the populace rise at once against the never-ending
    audacity of elected persons,
Where fierce men and women pour forth as the sea to the
    whistle of death pours its sweeping and unript waves,
Where outside authority enters always after the precedence
    of inside authority,
Where the citizen is always the head and ideal, and
    President, Mayor, Governor and what not, are agents
    for pay,

Where children are taught to be laws to themselves, and to
 depend on themselves,
Where equanimity is illustrated in affairs,
Where speculations on the soul are encouraged,
Where women walk in public processions in the streets the
 same as the men,
Where they enter the public assembly and take places the
 same as the men;
Where the city of the faithfulest friends stands,
Where the city of the cleanliness of the sexes stands,
Where the city of the healthiest fathers stands,
Where the city of the best-bodied mothers stands,
There the great city stands.

1

Over the Western sea hither from Niphon come,
Courteous, the swart-cheek'd two-sworded envoys,
Leaning back in their open barouches, bare-headed, impassive,
Ride to-day through Manhattan.

Libertad! I do not know whether others behold what I behold,
In the procession along with the nobles of Niphon, the
     errand-bearers,
Bringing up the rear, hovering above, around, or in the ranks
     marching,
But I will sing you a song of what I behold Libertad.

When million-footed Manhattan unpent descends to her
     pavements,
When the thunder-cracking guns arouse me with the proud
     roar I love,
When the round-mouth'd guns out of the smoke and smell
     I love spit their salutes,
When the fire-flashing guns have fully alerted me, and
     heaven-clouds canopy my city with a delicate thin haze,
When gorgeous the countless straight stems, the forests at
     the wharves, thicken with colors,
When every ship richly drest carries her flag at the peak,
When pennants trail and street-festoons hang from the
     windows,
When Broadway is entirely given up to foot-passengers and
     foot-standers, when the mass is densest,

When the façades of the houses are alive with people, when
    eyes gaze riveted tens of thousands at a time,
When the guests from the islands advance, when the pageant
    moves forward visible,
When the summons is made, when the answer that waited
    thousands of years answers,
I too arising, answering, descend to the pavements, merge
    with the crowd, and gaze with them.

2

Superb-faced Manhattan!
Comrade Americanos! to us, then at last the Orient comes.

To us, my city,
Where our tall-topt marble and iron beauties range on
    opposite sides, to walk in the space between,
To-day our Antipodes comes.

The Originatress comes,
The nest of languages, the bequeather of poems, the race
    of eld,
Florid with blood, pensive, rapt with musings, hot with
    passion,
Sultry with perfume, with ample and flowing garments,
With sunburnt visage, with intense soul and glittering eyes,
The race of Brahma comes.

See my cantabile! these and more are flashing to us from the
    procession,
As it moves changing, a kaleidoscope divine it moves
    changing before us.

For not the envoys nor the tann'd Japanee from his island
only,
Lithe and silent the Hindoo appears, the Asiatic continent
itself appears, the past, the dead,
The murky night-morning of wonder and fable inscrutable,
The envelop'd mysteries, the old and unknown hive-bees,
The north, the sweltering south, eastern Assyria, the
Hebrews, the ancient of ancients,
Vast desolated cities, the gliding present, all of these and
more are in the pageant-procession.

Geography, the world, is in it,
The Great Sea, the brood of islands, Polynesia, the coast
beyond,
The coast you henceforth are facing – you Libertad! from
your Western golden shores,
The countries there with their populations, the millions
en-masse are curiously here,
The swarming market-places, the temples with idols ranged
along the sides or at the end, bonze, brahmin, and
llama,
Mandarin, farmer, merchant, mechanic, and fisherman,
The singing-girl and the dancing-girl, the ecstatic persons,
the secluded emperors,
Confucius himself, the great poets and heroes, the warriors,
the castes, all,
Trooping up, crowding from all directions, from the Altay
mountains,
From Thibet, from the four winding and far-flowing rivers
of China,
From the southern peninsulas and the demi-continental
islands, from Malaysia,

These and whatever belongs to them palpable show forth to
    me, and are seiz'd by me,
And I am seiz'd by them, and friendlily held by them,
Till as here them all I chant, Libertad! for themselves and
    for you.

For I too raising my voice join the ranks of this pageant,
I am the chanter, I chant aloud over the pageant,
I chant the world on my Western sea,
I chant copious the islands beyond, thick as stars in the sky,
I chant the new empire grander than any before, as in a
    vision it comes to me,
I chant America the mistress, I chant a greater supremacy,
I chant projected a thousand blooming cities yet in time on
    those groups of sea-islands,
My sail-ships and steam-ships threading the archipelagoes,
My stars and stripes fluttering in the wind,
Commerce opening, the sleep of ages having done its work,
    races reborn, refresh'd,
Lives, works resumed – the object I know not – but the old,
    the Asiatic renew'd as it must be,
Commencing from this day surrounded by the world.

3

And you Libertad of the world!
You shall sit in the middle well-pois'd thousands and
    thousands of years,
As to-day from one side the nobles of Asia come to you,
As to-morrow from the other side the queen of England
    sends her eldest son to you.

The sign is reversing, the orb is enclosed,
The ring is circled, the journey is done,

The box-lid is but perceptibly open'd, nevertheless the
perfume pours copiously out of the whole box.

Young Libertad! with the venerable Asia, the all-mother,
Be considerate with her now and ever hot Libertad, for you
are all,
Bend your proud neck to the long-off mother now sending
messages over the archipelagoes to you,
Bend your proud neck low for once, young Libertad.

Were the children straying westward so long? so wide the
tramping?
Were the precedent dim ages debouching westward from
Paradise so long?
Were the centuries steadily footing it that way, all the while
unknown, for you, for reasons?

They are justified, they are accomplish'd, they shall now be
turn'd the other way also, to travel toward you thence,
They shall now also march obediently eastward for your
sake Libertad.

I sit and look out upon all the sorrows of the world, and
    upon all oppression and shame,
I hear secret convulsive sobs from young men at anguish
    with themselves, remorseful after deeds done,
I see in low life the mother misused by her children, dying,
    neglected, gaunt, desperate,
I see the wife misused by her husband, I see the treacherous
    seducer of young women,
I mark the ranklings of jealousy and unrequited love
    attempted to be hid, I see these sights on the earth,
I see the workings of battle, pestilence, tyranny, I see
    martyrs and prisoners,
I observe a famine at sea, I observe the sailors casting lots
    who shall be kill'd to preserve the lives of the rest,
I observe the slights and degradations cast by arrogant
    persons upon laborers, the poor, and upon negroes,
    and the like;
All these – all the meanness and agony without end I sitting
    look out upon,
See, hear, and am silent.

First O songs for a prelude,
Lightly strike on the stretch'd tympanum pride and joy in
    my city,
How she led the rest to arms, how she gave the cue,
How at once with lithe limbs unwaiting a moment she
    sprang,
(O superb! O Manhattan, my own, my peerless!
O strongest you in the hour of danger, in crisis! O truer
    than steel!)
How you sprang – how you threw off the costumes of peace
    with indifferent hand,
How your soft opera-music changed, and the drum and fife
    were heard in their stead,
How you led to the war, (that shall serve for our prelude,
    songs of soldiers,)
How Manhattan drum-taps led.

Forty years had I in my city seen soldiers parading,
Forty years as a pageant, till unawares the lady of this teeming
    and turbulent city,
Sleepless amid her ships, her houses, her incalculable wealth,
With her million children around her, suddenly,
At dead of night, at news from the south,
Incens'd struck with clinch'd hand the pavement.

A shock electric, the night sustain'd it,
Till with ominous hum our hive at daybreak pour'd out its
    myriads.

From the houses then and the workshops, and through all
the doorways,
Leapt they tumultuous, and lo! Manhattan arming.

To the drum-taps prompt,
The young men falling in and arming,
The mechanics arming, (the trowel, the jack-plane, the
blacksmith's hammer, tost aside with precipitation,)
The lawyer leaving his office and arming, the judge leaving
the court,
The driver deserting his wagon in the street, jumping
down, throwing the reins abruptly down on the horses'
backs,
The salesman leaving the store, the boss, book-keeper,
porter, all leaving;
Squads gather everywhere by common consent and arm,
The new recruits, even boys, the old men show them how
to wear their accoutrements, they buckle the straps
carefully,
Outdoors arming, indoors arming, the flash of the musket-
barrels,
The white tents cluster in camps, the arm'd sentries around,
the sunrise cannon and again at sunset,
Arm'd regiments arrive every day, pass through the city,
and embark from the wharves,
(How good they look as they tramp down to the river,
sweaty, with their guns on their shoulders!
How I love them! how I could hug them, with their brown
faces and their clothes and knapsacks cover'd with dust!)
The blood of the city up – arm'd! arm'd! the cry everywhere,

The flags flung out from the steeples of churches and from
    all the public buildings and stores,
The tearful parting, the mother kisses her son, the son
    kisses his mother,
(Loth is the mother to part, yet not a word does she speak to
    detain him,)
The tumultuous escort, the ranks of policemen preceding,
    clearing the way,
The unpent enthusiasm, the wild cheers of the crowd for
    their favorites,
The artillery, the silent cannons bright as gold, drawn along,
    rumble lightly over the stones,
(Silent cannons, soon to cease your silence,
Soon unlimber'd to begin the red business;)
All the mutter of preparation, all the determin'd arming,
The hospital service, the lint, bandages and medicines,
The women volunteering for nurses, the work begun for in
    earnest, no mere parade now;
War! an arm'd race is advancing! the welcome for battle, no
    turning away,
War! be it weeks, months, or years, an arm'd race is advancing
    to welcome it.

Mannahatta a-march – and it's O to sing it well!
It's O for a manly life in the camp.

And the sturdy artillery,
The guns bright as gold, the work for giants, to serve well
    the guns,
Unlimber them! (no more as the past forty years for salutes
    for courtesies merely,
Put in something now besides powder and wadding.)

And you lady of ships, you Mannahatta,
Old matron of this proud, friendly, turbulent city,
Often in peace and wealth you were pensive or covertly
    frown'd amid all your children,
But now you smile with joy exulting old Mannahatta.

YEAR THAT TREMBLED AND REEL'D BENEATH ME

Year that trembled and reel'd beneath me!
Your summer wind was warm enough, yet the air I breathed
    froze me,
A thick gloom fell through the sunshine and darken'd me,
Must I change my triumphant songs? said I to myself,
Must I indeed learn to chant the cold dirges of the baffled?
And sullen hymns of defeat?

LONG, TOO LONG AMERICA

Long, too long America,
Traveling roads all even and peaceful you learn'd from joys
    and prosperity only,
But now, ah now, to learn from crises of anguish, advancing,
    grappling with direst fate and recoiling not,
And now to conceive and show to the world what your
    children en-masse really are,
(For who except myself has yet conceiv'd what your
    children en-masse really are?

1

Give me the splendid silent sun with all his beams full-
     dazzling,
Give me juicy autumnal fruit ripe and red from the orchard,
Give me a field where the unmow'd grass grows,
Give me an arbor, give me the trellis'd grape,
Give me fresh corn and wheat, give me serene-moving
     animals teaching content,
Give me nights perfectly quiet as on high plateaus west of
     the Mississippi, and I looking up at the stars,
Give me odorous at sunrise a garden of beautiful flowers
     where I can walk undisturb'd,
Give me for marriage a sweet-breath'd woman of whom I
     should never tire,
Give me a perfect child, give me away aside from the noise
     of the world a rural domestic life,
Give me to warble spontaneous songs recluse by myself, for
     my own ears only,
Give me solitude, give me Nature, give me again O Nature
     your primal sanities!

These demanding to have them, (tired with ceaseless excite-
     ment, and rack'd by the war-strife,)
These to procure incessantly asking, rising in cries from my
     heart,
While yet incessantly asking still I adhere to my city,
Day upon day and year upon year O city, walking your
     streets,
Where you hold me enchain'd a certain time refusing to give
     me up,

Yet giving to make me glutted, enrich'd of soul, you give me
forever faces;
(O I see what I sought to escape, confronting, reversing my
cries,
I see my own soul trampling down what it ask'd for.)

2

Keep your splendid silent sun,
Keep your woods O Nature, and the quiet places by the
woods,
Keep your fields of clover and timothy, and your corn-fields
and orchards,
Keep the blossoming buckwheat fields where the Ninth-
month bees hum;
Give me faces and streets – give me these phantoms incessant
and endless along the trottoirs!
Give me interminable eyes – give me women – give me
comrades and lovers by the thousand!
Let me see new ones every day – let me hold new ones by
the hand every day!
Give me such shows – give me the streets of Manhattan!
Give me Broadway, with the soldiers marching – give me
the sound of the trumpets and drums!
(The soldiers in companies or regiments – some starting
away, flush'd and reckless,
Some, their time up, returning with thinn'd ranks, young,
yet very old, worn, marching, noticing nothing;)
Give me the shores and wharves heavy-fringed with black
ships!
O such for me! O an intense life, full to repletion and
varied!
The life of the theatre, bar-room, huge hotel, for me!

The saloon of the steamer! the crowded excursion for me!
   the torchlight procession!
The dense brigade bound for the war, with high piled military
   wagons following;
People, endless, streaming, with strong voices, passions,
   pageants,
Manhattan streets with their powerful throbs, with beating
   drums as now,
The endless and noisy chorus, the rustle and clank of muskets,
   (even the sight of the wounded,)
Manhattan crowds, with their turbulent musical chorus!
Manhattan faces and eyes forever for me.

Over the carnage rose prophetic a voice,
Be not dishearten'd, affection shall solve the problems of
     freedom yet,
Those who love each other shall become invincible,
They shall yet make Columbia victorious.

Sons of the Mother of All, you shall yet be victorious,
You shall yet laugh to scorn the attacks of all the remainder
     of the earth.

No danger shall balk Columbia's lovers,
If need be a thousand shall sternly immolate themselves for
     one.

One from Massachusetts shall be a Missourian's comrade,
From Maine and from hot Carolina, and another an
     Oregonese, shall be friends triune,
More precious to each other than all the riches of the earth.

To Michigan, Florida perfumes shall tenderly come,
Not the perfumes of flowers, but sweeter, and wafted
     beyond death.

It shall be customary in the houses and streets to see manly
     affection,
The most dauntless and rude shall touch face to face lightly,
The dependence of Liberty shall be lovers,
The continuance of Equality shall be comrades.

These shall tie you and band you stronger than hoops of
    iron,
I, ecstatic, O partners! O lands! with the love of lovers tie
    you.

(Were you looking to be held together by lawyers?
Or by an agreement on a paper? or by arms?
Nay, nor the world, nor any living thing, will so cohere.)

HOW SOLEMN AS ONE BY ONE

(*Washington City*, 1865)

How solemn as one by one,
As the ranks returning worn and sweaty, as the men file by
    where I stand,
As the faces the masks appear, as I glance at the faces studying
    the masks,
(As I glance upward out of this page studying you, dear
    friend, whoever you are,)
How solemn the thought of my whispering soul to each in
    the ranks, and to you,
I see behind each mask that wonder a kindred soul,
O the bullet could never kill what you really are, dear friend,
Nor the bayonet stab what you really are;
The soul! yourself I see, great as any, good as the best,
Waiting secure and content, which the bullet could never
    kill,
Nor the bayonet stab O friend.

REVERSALS

Let that which stood in front go behind,
Let that which was behind advance to the front,
Let bigots, fools, unclean persons, offer new propositions,
Let the old propositions be postponed,
Let a man seek pleasure everywhere except in himself,
Let a woman seek happiness everywhere except in herself.

THE CITY DEAD-HOUSE

By the city dead-house by the gate,
As idly sauntering wending my way from the clangor,
I curious pause, for lo, an outcast form, a poor dead prostitute
    brought,
Her corpse they deposit unclaim'd, it lies on the damp brick
    pavement,
The divine woman, her body, I see the body, I look on it
    alone,
That house once full of passion and beauty, all else I notice
    not,
Nor stillness so cold, nor running water from faucet, nor
    odors morbific impress me,
But the house alone – that wondrous house – that delicate
    fair house – that ruin!
That immortal house more than all the rows of dwellings
    ever built!
Or white-domed capitol with majestic figure surmounted,
    or all the old high-spired cathedrals,
That little house alone more than them all – poor, desperate
    house!
Fair, fearful wreck – tenement of a soul – itself a soul,
Unclaim'd, avoided house – take one breath from my
    tremulous lips,
Take one tear dropt aside as I go for thought of you,
Dead house of love – house of madness and sin, crumbled,
    crush'd,
House of life, erewhile talking and laughing – but ah, poor
    house, dead even then,
Months, years, an echoing, garnish'd house – but dead,
    dead, dead.

I WAS LOOKING A LONG WHILE

I was looking a long while for Intentions,
For a clew to the history of the past for myself, and for these
    chants – and now I have found it,
It is not in those paged fables in the libraries, (them I
    neither accept nor reject,)
It is no more in the legends than in all else,
It is in the present – it is this earth to-day,
It is in Democracy – (the purport and aim of all the past,)
It is the life of one man or one woman to-day – the average
    man of to-day,
It is in languages, social customs, literatures, arts,
It is in the broad show of artificial things, ships, machinery,
    politics, creeds, modern improvements, and the inter-
    change of nations,
All for the modern – all for the average man of to-day.

PRAYER OF COLUMBUS

A batter'd, wreck'd old man,
Thrown on this savage shore, far, far from home,
Pent by the sea and dark rebellious brows, twelve dreary
    months,
Sore, stiff with many toils, sicken'd and nigh to death,
I take my way along the island's edge,
Venting a heavy heart.

I am too full of woe!
Haply I may not live another day;
I cannot rest O God, I cannot eat or drink or sleep,
Till I put forth myself, my prayer, once more to Thee,
Breathe, bathe myself once more in Thee, commune with
    Thee,
Report myself once more to Thee.

Thou knowest my years entire, my life,
My long and crowded life of active work, not adoration
    merely;
Thou knowest the prayers and vigils of my youth,
Thou knowest my manhood's solemn and visionary
    meditations,
Thou knowest how before I commenced I devoted all to
    come to Thee,
Thou knowest I have in age ratified all those vows and
    strictly kept them,
Thou knowest I have not once lost nor faith nor ecstasy in
    Thee,
In shackles, prison'd, in disgrace, repining not,
Accepting all from Thee, as duly come from Thee.

All my emprises have been fill'd with Thee,
My speculations, plans, begun and carried on in thoughts of
     Thee,
Sailing the deep or journeying the land for Thee;
Intentions, purports, aspirations mine, leaving results to
     Thee.

O I am sure they really came from Thee,
The urge, the ardor, the unconquerable will,
The potent, felt, interior command, stronger than words,
A message from the Heavens whispering to me even in
     sleep,
These sped me on.

By me and these the work so far accomplish'd,
By me earth's elder cloy'd and stifled lands uncloy'd,
     unloos'd,
By me the hemispheres rounded and tied, the unknown to
     the known.

The end I know not, it is all in Thee,
Or small or great I know not – haply what broad fields, what
     lands,
Haply the brutish measureless human undergrowth I know,
Transplanted there may rise to stature, knowledge worthy
     Thee,
Haply the swords I know may there indeed be turn'd to
     reaping-tools,
Haply the lifeless cross I know, Europe's dead cross, may
     bud and blossom there.

One effort more, my altar this bleak sand;
That Thou O God my life hast lighted,

With ray of light, steady, ineffable, vouchsafed of Thee,
Light rare untellable, lighting the very light,
Beyond all signs, descriptions, languages;
For that O God, be it my latest word, here on my knees,
Old, poor, and paralyzed, I thank Thee.

My terminus near,
The clouds already closing in upon me,
The voyage balk'd, the course disputed, lost,
I yield my ships to Thee.

My hands, my limbs grow nerveless,
My brain feels rack'd, bewilder'd,
Let the old timbers part, I will not part,
I will cling fast to Thee, O God, though the waves buffet me,
Thee, Thee at least I know.

Is it the prophet's thought I speak, or am I raving?
What do I know of life? what of myself?
I know not even my own work past or present,
Dim ever-shifting guesses of it spread before me,
Of newer better worlds, their mighty parturition,
Mocking, perplexing me.

And these things I see suddenly, what mean they?
As if some miracle, some hand divine unseal'd my eyes,
Shadowy vast shapes smile through the air and sky,
And on the distant waves sail countless ships,
And anthems in new tongues I hear saluting me.

WHISPERS OF HEAVENLY DEATH

Whispers of heavenly death murmur'd I hear,
Labial gossip of night, sibilant chorals,
Footsteps gently ascending, mystical breezes wafted soft and
    low,
Ripples of unseen rivers, tides of a current flowing, forever
    flowing,
(Or is it the plashing of tears? the measureless waters of
    human tears?)

I see, just see skyward, great cloud-masses,
Mournfully slowly they roll, silently swelling and mixing,
With at times a half-dimm'd sadden'd far-off star,
Appearing and disappearing.

(Some parturition rather, some solemn immortal birth;
On the frontiers to eyes impenetrable,
Some soul is passing over.)

THE LAST INVOCATION

At the last, tenderly,
From the walls of the powerful fortress'd house,
From the clasp of the knitted locks, from the keep of the
    well-closed doors,
Let me be wafted.

Let me glide noiselessly forth;
With the key of softness unlock the locks – with a whisper,
Set ope the doors O soul.

Tenderly – be not impatient,
(Strong is your hold O mortal flesh,
Strong is your hold O love.)

Pensive and faltering,
The words *the Dead* I write,
For living are the Dead,
(Haply the only living, only real,
And I the apparition, I the spectre.)

MANNAHATTA

I was asking for something specific and perfect for my city,
Whereupon lo! upsprang the aboriginal name.

Now I see what there is in a name, a word, liquid, sane,
    unruly, musical, self-sufficient,
I see that the word of my city is that word from of old,
Because I see that word nested in nests of water-bays, superb,
Rich, hemm'd thick all around with sailships and steam-
    ships, an island sixteen miles long, solid-founded,
Numberless crowded streets, high growths of iron, slender,
    strong, light, splendidly uprising toward clear skies,
Tides swift and ample, well-loved by me, toward sundown,
The flowing sea-currents, the little islands, larger adjoining
    islands, the heights, the villas,
The countless masts, the white shore-steamers, the lighters,
    the ferry-boats, the black sea-steamers well-model'd,
The down-town streets, the jobbers' houses of business, the
    houses of business of the ship-merchants and money-
    brokers, the river-streets,
Immigrants arriving, fifteen or twenty thousand in a week,
The carts hauling goods, the manly race of drivers of
    horses, the brown-faced sailors,
The summer air, the bright sun shining, and the sailing
    clouds aloft,
The winter snows, the sleigh-bells, the broken ice in the
    river, passing along up or down with the flood-tide or
    ebb-tide,

The mechanics of the city, the masters, well-form'd, beautiful-faced, looking you straight in the eyes,

Trottoirs throng'd, vehicles, Broadway, the women, the shops and shows,

A million people – manners free and superb – open voices – hospitality – the most courageous and friendly young men,

City of hurried and sparkling waters! city of spires and masts!

City nested in bays! my city!

A CLEAR MIDNIGHT

This is thy hour O Soul, thy free flight into the wordless,
Away from books, away from art, the day erased, the lesson
    done,
Thee fully forth emerging, silent, gazing, pondering the
    themes thou lovest best,
Night, sleep, death and the stars.

THOUGHTS

I

Of these years I sing,
How they pass and have pass'd through convuls'd pains, as
    through parturitions,
How America illustrates birth, muscular youth, the promise,
    the sure fulfilment, the absolute success, despite of
    people – illustrates evil as well as good,
The vehement struggle so fierce for unity in one's-self;
How many hold despairingly yet to the models departed,
    caste, myths, obedience, compulsion, and to infidelity,
How few see the arrived models, the athletes, the Western
    States, or see freedom or spirituality, or hold any faith
    in results,
(But I see the athletes, and I see the results of the war glorious
    and inevitable, and they again leading to other results.)

How the great cities appear – how the Democratic masses,
    turbulent, wilful, as I love them,
How the whirl, the contest, the wrestle of evil with good,
    the sounding and resounding, keep on and on,
How society waits unform'd, and is for a while between
    things ended and things begun,
How America is the continent of glories, and of the triumph
    of freedom and of the Democracies, and of the fruits of
    society, and of all that is begun,
And how the States are complete in themselves – and how
    all triumphs and glories are complete in themselves, to
    lead onward,

And how these of mine and of the States will in their turn be
    convuls'd, and serve other parturitions and transitions,
And how all people, sights, combinations, the democratic
    masses too, serve – and how every fact, and war itself,
    with all its horrors, serves,
And how now or at any time each serves the exquisite
    transition of death.

2

Of seeds dropping into the ground, of births,
Of the steady concentration of America, inland, upward,
    to impregnable and swarming places,
Of what Indiana, Kentucky, Arkansas, and the rest, are
    to be,
Of what a few years will show there in Nebraska, Colorado,
    Nevada, and the rest,
(Or afar, mounting the Northern Pacific to Sitka or Aliaska,)
Of what the feuillage of America is the preparation for – and
    of what all sights, North, South, East and West, are,
Of this Union welded in blood, of the solemn price paid,
    of the unnamed lost ever present in my mind;
Of the temporary use of materials for identity's sake,
Of the present, passing, departing – of the growth of
    completer men than any yet,
Of all sloping down there where the fresh free giver the
    mother, the Mississippi flows,
Of mighty inland cities yet unsurvey'd and unsuspected,
Of the new and good names, of the modern developments,
    of inalienable homesteads,
Of a free and original life there, of simple diet and clean and
    sweet blood,

Of litheness, majestic faces, clear eyes, and perfect physique
there,
Of immense spiritual results future years far West, each side
of the Anahuacs,
Of these songs, well understood there, (being made for that
area,)
Of the native scorn of grossness and gain there,
(O it lurks in me night and day – what is gain after all to
savageness and freedom?)

THE SOBBING OF THE BELLS

(Midnight, Sept. 19–20, 1881)

The sobbing of the bells, the sudden death-news every-
    where,
The slumberers rouse, the rapport of the People,
(Full well they know that message in the darkness,
Full well return, respond within their breasts, their brains,
    the sad reverberations,)
The passionate toll and clang – city to city, joining, sounding,
    passing,
Those heart-beats of a Nation in the night.

SO LONG!

To conclude, I announce what comes after me.

I remember I said before my leaves sprang at all,
I would raise my voice jocund and strong with reference to
    consummations.

When America does what was promis'd,
When through these States walk a hundred millions of
    superb persons,
When the rest part away for superb persons and contribute
    to them,
When breeds of the most perfect mothers denote America,
Then to me and mine our due fruition.

I have press'd through in my own right,
I have sung the body and the soul, war and peace have I
    sung, and the songs of life and death,
And the songs of birth, and shown that there are many
    births.

I have offer'd my style to every one, I have journey'd with
    confident step;
While my pleasure is yet at the full I whisper *So long!*
And take the young woman's hand and the young man's
    hand for the last time.

I announce natural persons to arise,
I announce justice triumphant,
I announce uncompromising liberty and equality,

I announce the justification of candor and the justification
of pride.

I announce that the identity of these States is a single
identity only,
I announce the Union more and more compact, indissoluble,
I announce splendors and majesties to make all the previous
politics of the earth insignificant.

I announce adhesiveness, I say it shall be limitless,
unloosen'd,
I say you shall yet find the friend you were looking for.

I announce a man or woman coming, perhaps you are the
one, (*So long!*)
I announce the great individual, fluid as Nature, chaste,
affectionate, compassionate, fully arm'd.

I announce a life that shall be copious, vehement, spiritual,
bold,
I announce an end that shall lightly and joyfully meet its
translation.

I announce myriads of youths, beautiful, gigantic, sweet-
blooded,
I announce a race of splendid and savage old men.

O thicker and faster – (*So long!*)
O crowding too close upon me,
I foresee too much, it means more than I thought,
It appears to me I am dying.

Hasten throat and sound your last,
Salute me – salute the days once more. Peal the old cry once
more.

Screaming electric, the atmosphere using,
At random glancing, each as I notice absorbing,
Swiftly on, but a little while alighting,
Curious envelop'd messages delivering,
Sparkles hot, seed ethereal down in the dirt dropping,
Myself unknowing, my commission obeying, to question it
never daring,
To ages and ages yet the growth of the seed leaving,
To troops out of the war arising, they the tasks I have set
promulging,
To women certain whispers of myself bequeathing, their
affection me more clearly explaining,
To young men my problems offering – no dallier I – I the
muscle of their brains trying,
So I pass, a little time vocal, visible, contrary,
Afterward a melodious echo, passionately bent for, (death
making me really undying,)
The best of me then when no longer visible, for toward that
I have been incessantly preparing.

What is there more, that I lag and pause and crouch
extended with unshut mouth?
Is there a single final farewell?

My songs cease, I abandon them,
From behind the screen where I hid I advance personally
solely to you.

Camerado, this is no book,
Who touches this touches a man,
(Is it night? are we here together alone?)
It is I you hold and who holds you,
I spring from the pages into your arms – decease calls me
    forth.

O how your fingers drowse me,
Your breath falls around me like dew, your pulse lulls the
    tympans of my ears,
I feel immerged from head to foot,
Delicious, enough.

Enough O deed impromptu and secret,
Enough O gliding present – enough O summ'd-up past.

Dear friend whoever you are take this kiss,
I give it especially to you, do not forget me,
I feel like one who has done work for the day to retire awhile,
I receive now again of my many translations, from my
    avataras ascending, while others doubtless await me,
An unknown sphere more real than I dream'd, more direct,
    darts awakening rays about me, *So long!*
Remember my words, I may again return,
I love you, I depart from materials,
I am as one disembodied, triumphant, dead.

MANNAHATTA

My city's fit and noble name resumed,
Choice aboriginal name, with marvellous beauty, meaning,
A rocky founded island – shores where ever gayly dash the coming,
going, hurrying sea waves.

AMERICA

Centre of equal daughters, equal sons,
All, all alike endear'd, grown, ungrown, young or old,
Strong, ample, fair, enduring, capable, rich,
Perennial with the Earth, with Freedom, Law and Love,
A grand, sane, towering, seated Mother,
Chair'd in the adamant of Time.

BROADWAY

What hurrying human tides, or day or night!
What passions, winnings, losses, ardors, swim thy waters!
What whirls of evil, bliss and sorrow, stem thee!
What curious questioning glances – glints of love!
Leer, envy, scorn, contempt, hope, aspiration!
Thou portal – thou arena – thou of the myriad long-drawn
    lines and groups!
(Could but thy flagstones, curbs, façades, tell their
    inimitable tales;
Thy windows rich, and huge hotels – thy side-walks wide;)
Thou of the endless sliding, mincing, shuffling feet!
Thou, like the parti-colored world itself – like infinite,
    teeming, mocking life!
Thou visor'd, vast, unspeakable show and lesson!

Ever the undiscouraged, resolute, struggling soul of man;
(Have former armies fail'd? then we send fresh armies – and
    fresh again;)
Ever the grappled mystery of all earth's ages old or new;
Ever the eager eyes, hurrahs, the welcome-clapping hands,
    the loud applause;
Ever the soul dissatisfied, curious, unconvinced at last;
Struggling to-day the same – battling the same.

TRUE CONQUERORS

Old farmers, travelers, workmen (no matter how crippled
    or bent,)
Old sailors, out of many a perilous voyage, storm and wreck,
Old soldiers from campaigns, with all their wounds, defeats
    and scars;
Enough that they've survived at all – long life's unflinching
    ones!
Forth from their struggles, trials, fights, to have emerged at
    all – in that alone,
True conquerors o'er all the rest.

Here first the duties of to-day, the lessons of the concrete,
Wealth, order, travel, shelter, products, plenty;
As of the building of some varied, vast, perpetual edifice,
Whence to arise inevitable in time, the towering roofs,
    the lamps,
The solid-planted spires tall shooting to the stars.

STRONGER LESSONS

Have you learn'd lessons only of those who admired you,
    and were tender with you, and stood aside for you?
Have you not learn'd great lessons from those who reject
    you, and brace themselves against you? or who treat you
    with contempt, or dispute the passage with you?

LONG, LONG HENCE

After a long, long course, hundreds of years, denials,
Accumulations, rous'd love and joy and thought,
Hopes, wishes, aspirations, ponderings, victories, myriads
    of readers,
Coating, compassing, covering – after ages' and ages'
    encrustations,
Then only may these songs reach fruition.

THE COMMONPLACE

The commonplace I sing;
How cheap is health! how cheap nobility!
Abstinence, no falsehood, no gluttony, lust;
The open air I sing, freedom, toleration,
(Take here the mainest lesson – less from books – less from
    the schools,)
The common day and night – the common earth and waters,
Your farm – your work, trade, occupation,
The democratic wisdom underneath, like solid ground for all.

One thought ever at the fore –
That in the Divine Ship, the World, breasting Time and
    Space,
All Peoples of the globe together sail, sail the same voyage,
    are bound to the same destination.

WHILE BEHIND ALL FIRM AND ERECT

While behind all, firm and erect as ever,
Undismay'd amid the rapids – amid the irresistible and
    deadly urge,
Stands a helmsman, with brow elate and strong hand.

A THOUGHT OF COLUMBUS

The mystery of mysteries, the crude and hurried ceaseless
    flame, spontaneous, bearing on itself.
The bubble and the huge, round, concrete orb!
A breath of Deity, as thence the bulging universe unfolding!
The many issuing cycles from their precedent minute!
The eras of the soul incepting in an hour,
Haply the widest, farthest evolutions of the world and man.

Thousands and thousands of miles hence, and now four
    centuries back,
A mortal impulse thrilling its brain cell,
Reck'd or unreck'd, the birth can no longer be postpon'd:
A phantom of the moment, mystic, stalking, sudden,
Only a silent thought, yet toppling down of more than walls
    of brass or stone.
(A flutter at the darkness' edge as if old Time's and Space's
    secret near revealing.)
A thought! a definite thought works out in shape.
Four hundred years roll on.
The rapid cumulus – trade, navigation, war, peace,
    democracy, roll on;
The restless armies and the fleets of time following their
    leader – the old camps of ages pitch'd in newer, larger
    areas,
The tangl'd, long-deferr'd eclaircissement of human life
    and hopes boldly begins untying,
As here to-day up-grows the Western World.

(An added word yet to my song, far Discoverer, as ne'er
    before sent back to son of earth –
If still thou hearest, hear me,
Voicing as now – lands, races, arts, bravas to thee,
O'er the long backward path to thee – one vast consensus,
    north, south, east, west,
Soul plaudits! acclamation! reverent echoes!
One manifold, huge memory to thee! oceans and lands!
The modern world to thee and thought of thee!)

Anvil Press Poetry

publishes a wide range of contemporary poetry in English, new translations of classic and modern poetry from many languages, and other work related to poetry. For a full list of our publications, please see our website.

WWW.ANVILPRESSPOETRY.COM